Quotable
KING

Quotable
KING

Words of Wisdom, Inspiration,
and Freedom by and about
Dr. Martin Luther King Jr.,
One of America's Great Civil Rights Leaders

Steve Eubanks

TowleHouse Publishing
Nashville, Tennessee

TowleHouse books are distributed by National Book Network
(NBN), 4720 Boston Way, Lanham, Maryland 20706.

Library of Congress Cataloging-in-Publication data is available.
ISBN: 1-931249-11-3

Cover design by Gore Studio, Inc.
Page design by Mike Towle

Printed in the United States of America
1 2 3 4 5 6 — 06 05 04 03 02

CONTENTS

To Martin Luther King Jr. and the Movement.

PREFACE

Amid the cries of an oppressed people, one voice rose up above all others. The words and deeds of Reverend Martin Luther King, Jr. aroused a people to action, not revolutionary action or violent action, but nonviolent social civil disobedience, the kind of actions that stirred a nation to rectify an injustice and opened the eyes of the world to the moral principals of racial equality. Those words of inspiration should forever be remembered and embraced.

INTRODUCTION

For anyone younger than forty years of age, it's hard to imagine a time in America when men and women of different races couldn't eat lunch together, couldn't drink from the same water fountain, couldn't use the same rest rooms, or stay in the same hotels. So foreign are these ideas to today's middle-aged generation and all those thereafter that the mind plays tricks; segregated schools and "colored" water coolers are lumped in the same mental box with slave auctions of the eighteenth century and depression-era lynchings of the Old South. It seems unfathomable that men and women of color had to give up their bus seats to Anglo-Saxon Americans as recently as 1960. It's impossible to visualize men being beaten for ordering a hamburger at a "white only" lunch counter in our lifetime. The framed images—grainy and colorless—hang like fossilized footprints, and the moving clips—faded and jerky, replayed on PBS specials—are viewed as chin-rubbing historical artifacts, as ancient and arcane as ox-drawn carts and outhouses.

The older generation, now as gray as the images from that bygone era, can only shake their heads and wonder. For them the memories are like yesterday, and the term "the Struggle" needs no further explanation. They were the ones standing up to the oppression, the bigotry, the violence, and the shameful scourge of segregation. It was they who risked life and limb for the basic rights to vote, to worship, to walk and to eat and to live as free men and women in America. Their cause was that of decency, fairness, and basic human rights, the inspiring principles Thomas Jefferson had penned almost two centuries before when he wrote that "all men are created equal, endowed by their Creator with certain inalienable rights, among those, life, liberty, and the pursuit of happiness."

Liberty and happiness were long in coming for men of color in America. But through the words and deeds of one inspiring figure, the Struggle became a cause, and the cause grew into a movement. By the summer of 1963, everyone in America knew the name of the Montgomery minister whose words inspired a people to seek justice. Martin Luther King Jr., an Atlanta native and son of a Baptist preacher, personified the courage and conviction of the Struggle. His gifted oratorical skills, his moral courage, his command presence, and his indefatigable spirit inspired the world and changed a nation.

America looks much different today than it did forty years ago. Two generations of white and black Americans have sat side by side in classrooms from kindergarten through college. Black and white coworkers dine out wherever they please. Planes, trains, and buses are racially neutral; and offices, factories, loading docks, restaurants, libraries, sporting arenas, museums, manicured neighborhoods with common playgrounds, and cruise ships to Saint Bart are all integrated. Forty years after Dr. King burst onto the scene with his message of nonviolent civil disobedience, we are closer than ever to his dream of a day when "men are judged not by the color of their skin but by the content of their character."

We've come a long way. We still have a long way to go. Since the days when Dr. King traveled the world and gave hundreds of speeches a year, we have had two African Americans serve on the United States Supreme Court. Dozens more have served in Congress, while hundreds have served in state and local governments. African American mayors have governed New York, San Francisco, Atlanta, Houston, Dallas, and Detroit, among others, and more minorities serve in the top echelons of corporate America than at any time in our nation's history. Even though we still have differences, we discuss our differences civilly and work toward solutions together because of the leadership model Dr. King provided in his thirty-nine short years on this planet.

The legacy of Dr. King has now lived almost as long as the man himself walked the earth. Remembering his words is a part of that legacy. And it is the duty of those who seek justice and honor and nobility in the American Dream to never forget.

Quotable
KING

SEGREGATION

THE SIGNS OF THE TIMES IN THE FORTIES AND FIFTIES WERE CLEAR. "WHITE ONLY" MONIKERS DONNED THE DOORS OF ESTABLISHMENTS ALL OVER AMERICA, AND SEGREGATION REMAINED ENTRENCHED POLICY THROUGHOUT MOST OF SOCIETY. POLITICIANS, SCHOOL PRINCIPALS, AND EVEN PASTORS FROM THEIR PULPITS BEAT THE DRUMS OF SEGREGATION AND STIRRED THE FLAMES OF HATRED TOWARD ANYONE WHO OPPOSED THEIR VIEWS. IT WAS A TIME OF GREAT CONFLICT, AND A TIME OF GREAT RESOLVE.

I could never adjust to the separate waiting rooms, separate eating places, (and) separate rest rooms, partly because the separate was always unequal, and partly because the very idea of separation did something to my sense of dignity and self-respect.[1]

Who are we? We are the descendants of slaves . . . we are the heirs of a past of rope, fire, and murder. I for one am not ashamed of this past.[2]

⸺⸎⸺

My mother took me on her lap and began telling me about slavery and how it ended with the Civil War. She tried to explain the divided system of the South . . . as a social condition rather than a natural order.[3]

⸺⸎⸺

The American Negro is neither totally African nor totally Western. He is Afro-American, a true hybrid, a combination of two cultures.[4]

⸺⸎⸺

A doctrine of black supremacy is as evil as a doctrine of white supremacy.[5]

⸺⸎⸺

Now is the time to lift our national policy from the quicksand of racial injustice to the solid rock of human dignity.[6]

—⁂—

We can get rid of segregation in most areas of American life by 1963.[7]

—spoken by King in 1956 and before the Civil Rights Acts of 1957 and 1964

—⁂—

Segregation scars the soul of both the segregator and the segregated. The segregator looks upon the segregated as a thing to be used, not a person to be respected.[8]

—⁂—

Segregation denies the sacredness of human personality.[9]

—⁂—

Two segregated souls never meet in God.[10]

—⁂—

HE WAS THE MAN, MORE THAN ANY OTHER OF HIS
GENERATION, WHO GAZED UPON THE GREAT WALL OF
SEGREGATION AND SAW THAT IT COULD BE DESTROYED
BY THE POWER OF LOVE.[11]

—*Jimmy Carter*

Segregation is morally wrong and sinful.[12]

Genuine integration will come when men are obedient
to the unenforceable.[13]

Segregation is also morally wrong because it deprives
man of freedom, that quality which makes him a man.[14]

While abhorring segregation, we shall love the segregationist. This is the only way to create the beloved
community.[15]

King (in back) joins others, including Ralph Abernathy (front left), on bus ride soon after the Supreme Court's integration order went into effect in 1956. (AP/Wide World photo)

FAITH

"WITHOUT FAITH I AM NOTHING" WERE THE WORDS OF THE APOSTLE PAUL. THOSE WORDS WERE ECHOED MANY TIMES BY DR. KING. WHETHER THROWING HIS HEAD BACK AND SINGING "I WANT TO BE MORE LIKE JESUS" AS PART OF THE EBENEZER BAPTIST CHURCH CHOIR, PREACHING FROM THE PULPIT IN MONT-GOMERY, OR WRITING FROM A JAIL CELL IN BIRMINGHAM, KING RELIED ON HIS UNDYING FAITH IN CHRIST FOR HIS STRENGTH. FOR WITHOUT IT, HE KNEW HE AND HIS CAUSE WOULD BE NOTHING.

We must be reminded anew that God is at work in His universe. He is not outside the world looking on with a sort of cold indifference.[1]

As we struggle to defeat the forces of evil, the God of the universe struggles with us.[2]

A just law is a manmade code that squares with the moral law or the law of God. An unjust law is a code that is out of harmony with the moral law.[3]

The greatness of our God lies in the fact that he is both tough-minded and tenderhearted.[4]

God has two outstretched arms. One is strong enough to surround us with justice, and one is gentle enough to embrace us with grace.[5]

IN HIM THE WORD BECAME FLESH AND DWELT AMONG MEN.[6]
—*Jesse Jackson*

I don't know what will happen; I don't know where the money will come from. But I have to make a faith act.[7]
—*King after finding out the SCLC had run out of bail money just prior to the Good Friday march on Birmingham city hall in 1963*

Whenever you set out to build a temple, you must face the fact that there is a tension at the heart of the universe between good and evil.[8]

God, who gave us minds for thinking and bodies for working, would defeat his own purpose if he permitted us to obtain through prayer what may come through work and intelligence.[9]

God freely offers to do for us what we cannot do for ourselves. Our humble and openhearted acceptance is faith. So by faith we are saved.[10]

There have been times that I have been carried out of myself by something greater than myself, and to that something I give myself. Has the great something been God?[11]

—*King writing as a seminary student*

There is a creative force that works to pull down mountains of evil and level hilltops of injustice. God still works through history His wonders to perform.[12]

From my background I gained my regulating Christian ideals. From Gandhi I learned my operational technique.[13]

I have felt the power of God transforming the fatigue of despair into the buoyancy of hope.[14]

If we are to go forward today, we've got to go back and rediscover some mighty precious values that we've left behind.[15]

All reality hinges on moral foundations.[16]

———

It's possible to affirm the existence of God with your lips and deny his existence with your life.[17]

———

I'm not going to put my ultimate faith in the little gods that can be destroyed in an atomic age but the God who has been our help in ages past.[18]

———

God is neither a Baptist nor a Methodist; He is neither a Presbyterian nor an Episcopalian. God is bigger than all of our denominations.[19]

———

You must face the tragic fact that when you stand at eleven on Sunday morning to sing "All Hail the Power of Jesus' Name" and "Dear Lord and Father of All Mankind," you stand in the most segregated hour of Christian America.[20]

———

In Christ there is neither Jew nor Gentile, there is neither bond nor free, there is neither male nor female, for we are all one in Christ Jesus.[21]

—*King quoting Gal. 3:28 (King James version)*

God is a living God. In Him there is feeling and will, responsive to the deepest yearnings of the human heart: *this* God both evokes and answers prayers.[22]

God is a living God. In Him there is feeling and will,

———⟨⟩———

Behind the harsh appearance of the world there is a benign power.[23]

———⟨⟩———

We must admit that there is some mystery surrounding God's being. There are certain things that happen in our lives and in the life of the universe that we can't explain in rational terms. You must live by the faith that all suffering has some purpose which the finite mind of man can never comprehend.[24]

———⟨⟩———

Death is not the ultimate evil; the ultimate evil is to be outside God's love. We need not join the mad rush to purchase an earthly fallout shelter. God is our eternal fallout shelter.[25]

———⟨⟩———

The Christian faith makes it possible for us nobly to accept that which cannot be changed, and to meet disappointments and sorrow with an inner poise, and to absorb the most intense pain without abandoning our sense of hope.[26]

Christianity clearly affirms that in the long struggle between good and evil, good eventually will emerge as victor.[27]

I do not think God approves the death penalty for any crime—rape and murder included. God's concern is to improve individuals and bring them to the point of conversion.[28]

MARTIN LUTHER KING JR. WAS THE CONSCIENCE OF HIS GENERATION. HE WAS A DOCTOR TO A SICK SOCIETY. HE WAS A PROPHET TO A NEW AND BETTER AMERICA.[29]

—*Jimmy Carter*

Ultimately one is changed by totally surrendering his will to God's will. You cannot solve the problems alone.[30]

EDUCATION

CIVIL DISOBEDIENCE WASN'T A NORMAL PART OF THE EDUCATIONAL CURRICULUM AT ANY OF THE INSTITUTIONS KING ATTENDED. BUT HIS VORACIOUS APPETITE FOR LEARNING LED HIM TO READ AND STUDY PHILOSOPHIES OUTSIDE THE NORMALLY ASSIGNED COURSE WORK. HE WAS A BRILLIANT STUDENT AND A QUICK STUDY WHO FINISHED HIGH SCHOOL TWO YEARS EARLY AND ENROLLED AT MOREHOUSE COLLEGE AT AGE FIFTEEN.

When I went to Atlanta's Morehouse College as a freshman in 1944, my concern for racial and economic justice was already substantial. During my student days at Morehouse I read Thoreau's *Essay on Civil Disobedience* for the first time. Fascinated by the idea of refusing to cooperate with an evil system, I was so deeply moved that I reread the work several times. This was my first intellectual contact with the theory of nonviolent resistance.[1]

Remember that education gives you not only knowledge, which is power, but wisdom, which is control.[2]

———

Education is more than ever the passport to decent economic positions.[3]

———

Parents should be involved in the schools to a much greater extent, breaking down the barriers between professionals and the community that they serve.[4]

———

The road to effective education requires helping teachers to teach more effectively.[5]

—⊷⊶—

Education without social action is a one-sided value because it has no true power potential. Social action without education is a weak expression of pure energy.[6]

—⊷⊶—

Deeds uninformed by educated thought can take false directions. When we go into action and confront our adversaries, we must be as armed with knowledge as they.[7]

—⊷⊶—

Education is too important today to be left to profession-al fads and needs.[8]

—⊷⊶—

King and other leaders link arms as they help lead the March on Washington in August 1963. (AP/Wide World photo)

Schools have to be infused with a mission if they are to be successful.[9]

—⚬—

The job of the school is to teach so well that family background is no longer an issue.[10]

—⚬—

Study constantly even after you leave high school and college.[11]

—⚬—

We must remember that intelligence is not enough. Intelligence plus character—that is the goal of true education.[12]

—⚬—

GANDHI

KING WAS A STUDENT AT CROZER THEOLOGICAL SEMINARY IN PENNSYLVANIA WHEN HE FIRST STUDIED THE WRITINGS AND PHILOSOPHICAL TEACHINGS OF INDIA'S MAHATMA GANDHI. STRUCK BY THE GREAT LEADER'S COMMITMENT TO NONVIOLENT SOCIAL CHANGE, AND THE IMPACT IT HAD IN LEADING TO INDIAN INDEPENDENCE FROM GREAT BRITAIN, KING COMMITTED HIMSELF TO A SIMILAR APPROACH OF STRENGTH AND CHANGE THROUGH LOVE AND NONVIOLENT RESISTANCE. IN THE DUE COURSE OF HISTORY, KING AND GANDHI HAVE IN A SENSE BECOME SYNONYMOUS WITH EACH OTHER.

What was new about Mahatma Gandhi's movement in India was that he mounted a revolution on hope and love, hope and nonviolence.[1]

⸺⟊⟊⸺

Gandhi was probably the first person in history to lift the love ethic of Jesus above mere interaction between individuals to a powerful and effective social force on a large scale.[2]

⸺⟊⟊⸺

Love for Gandhi was a potent instrument for social and collective transformation.[3]

———⚬———

My study of Gandhi convinced me that true pacifism is not nonresistance to evil but nonviolent resistance to evil.[4]

———⚬———

Christ furnished the spirit and motivation, while Gandhi furnished the method.[5]

———⚬———

Gandhi resisted evil with as much vigor and power as the violent resister, but he resisted with love instead of hate.[6]

CORETTA

MARRIED IN 1953, MARTIN AND CORETTA
KING VENTURED ON A JOURNEY NO ONE
COULD HAVE POSSIBLY IMAGINED AT THE
TIME. THROUGH ALL THE TRIALS AND
TRIBULATIONS, THE DEATH THREATS, THE
INSULTS, THE SEEMINGLY ENDLESS TRAV-
ELS, AND, IN THE END, THE ASSASSINA-
TION, CORETTA WAS MARTIN'S BIGGEST
ADVOCATE, HIS STRONGEST SUPPORTER,
HIS ROCK, AND HIS STRENGTH. MORE
THAN THREE DECADES AFTER HIS DEATH,
SHE REMAINS HIS MOST VIGILANT
DEFENDER.

I am indebted to my wife Coretta, without whose love, sacrifices, and loyalty neither life nor work would bring fulfillment. She has given me words of consolation when I needed them and a well-ordered home where Christian love is a reality.[1]

My devoted wife has been a constant source of consolation to me through all the difficulties. In the midst of the most tragic experiences, she never became panicky or overemotional.[2]

My wife was always stronger than I was through the struggle. While she had certain natural fears and anxieties concerning my welfare, she never allowed them to hamper my active participation in the movement.[3]

Many times Coretta saw her good meals grow dry in the oven when a sudden emergency kept me away. Yet she never complained, and she was always there when I needed her.[4]

King, flanked by Coretta, shakes hands with fellow reverend Ralph Abernathy just after King had been found guilty of leading the Montgomery bus boycott in March 1956. (AP/Wide World photo)

CIVIL RIGHTS MOVEMENT

A YEAR AFTER KING MOVED HIS FAMILY TO MONTGOMERY SO HE COULD BEGIN HIS PASTORSHIP OF THE DEXTER AVENUE BAPTIST CHURCH, THE CIVIL RIGHTS MOVEMENT WAS BORN. ON DECEMBER 1, 1955, ROSA PARKS WAS ARRESTED FOR FAILING TO GIVE UP HER SEAT ON A CITY BUS TO A WHITE MAN. AN ENSUING BOYCOTT OF THE MONTGOMERY CITY BUSES BROUGHT THE CITY'S TRANSPORTATION DEPARTMENT TO A VIRTUAL STANDSTILL. KING WAS AT THE CENTER OF THE BOYCOTT, LEADING FROM HIS PULPIT AND FROM THE BACK ROOMS OF A MOVEMENT IN ITS INFANCY.

If you will protest courageously, and yet with dignity and Christian love, when the history books are written in future generations, the historians will have to pause and say, "There lived a great people—a black people—who injected new meaning and dignity into the veins of civilization."[1]

IN THE LIFE OF MARTIN LUTHER KING JR., OUR BLACK
CITIZENS OF GEORGIA AND THROUGHOUT THIS NATION SAW
THEIR OWN ASPIRATIONS REALIZED, AND THEY SAW THE
PREJUDICES AND LEGAL PROHIBITION AGAINST FULL CITIZEN-
SHIP BEGIN TO BE REMOVED. THE PRIVILEGED AND POWERFUL
LEADERS OF OUR NATION SAID, "THIS CANNOT BE."[2]

—Jimmy Carter

THE COUNTRY BELONGS TO YOU AS MUCH AS TO ME; YOU
CAN DETERMINE WHAT'S BEST JUST AS WELL AS I CAN. BUT
DON'T MAKE STATEMENTS THAT SOUND LIKE A THREAT.
THAT'S NOT THE WAY TO DEAL WITH US.[3]

*—Bobby Kennedy in a phone conversation with King following the
arrest of the Freedom Riders in Jackson, Mississippi, in 1963*

King's response to Kennedy:
It's difficult to understand the position of oppressed people.
Ours is a way out: creative, moral, and nonviolent . . . It
can save the soul of America. You must understand that
we've made no gains without pressure, and I hope that
pressure will always be moral, legal, and peaceful.[4]

There comes a time when people get tired of being trampled over by the iron feet of oppression.[5]

―――

I DON'T REALLY KNOW WHY I WOULDN'T MOVE. THERE WAS NO PLOT OR PLAN AT ALL. I WAS JUST TIRED FROM SHOPPING. MY FEET HURT.[6]

—*Rosa Parks*

―――

Freedom is not won by a passive acceptance of suffering. Freedom is won by a struggle *against* suffering.[7]

―――

It is one of the splendid ironies of our day that Montgomery, the Cradle of the Confederacy, is being transformed into Montgomery, the cradle of freedom and justice.[8]

―――

There is amazing power in unity. Where there is true unity, every effort to disunite only serves to strengthen the unity.[9]

―――

We must not let the fact that we are the victims of injustice lull us into abrogating responsibility for our own lives.[10]

———

KING WAS FRESH, A NEWCOMER, YOUNG, ARTICULATE, KNOWLEDGEABLE, HIGHLY EDUCATED, AND HAD NOT IDENTIFIED HIMSELF WITH ANY COMMUNITY ACTIVITIES OTHER THAN CHURCH.[11]

—*Fred Gray, King's first civil rights attorney*

———

HE WAS ENTIRELY COMFORTABLE AND SECURE IN THE ROLE HE KNEW HE HAD . . . HE WAS THE UNDISPUTED LEADER, THE UNDISPUTED SYMBOL OF WHAT THE MOVEMENT HAD COME TO.[12]

—*John Lewis, U.S. representative and longtime civil rights activist*

———

NOW THE TIME HAS COME FOR THIS NATION TO FULFILL ITS PROMISE. THE EVENTS IN BIRMINGHAM AND ELSEWHERE HAVE SO INCREASED THE CRIES FOR EQUALITY THAT NO CITY OR STATE LEGISLATIVE BODY CAN CHOOSE TO IGNORE THEM.[13]

—*John F. Kennedy*

———

THE SCLC

THE THIRTEEN-MONTH MONTGOMERY BUS
BOYCOTT PROPELLED KING TO NATIONAL
PROMINENCE. TO THE WHITE CIRCLES OF
THE SEGREGATIONIST SOUTH, HE WAS A VILE
AGITATOR DETERMINED TO UNDERMINE THE
SOCIAL FABRIC OF THE NATION. BUT FOR
MINORITIES, HE WAS A HERO, A CHAMPION,
A CRUSADER, AND A FRIEND. IN 1957,
PROPELLED BY THE SUCCESS AND RECOGNI-
TION HE HAD RECEIVED IN MONTGOMERY,
KING ASSEMBLED SIXTY BLACK MINISTERS IN
NEW ORLEANS AND FORMED THE SOUTHERN
CHRISTIAN LEADERSHIP CONFERENCE. THE
CHARTER MISSION OF THE SCLC WAS TO
"SAVE THE SOUL OF AMERICA" THROUGH
OPPOSITION TO SEGREGATIONIST POLICIES.
THROUGHOUT THE FIFTIES AND SIXTIES,
THE SCLC WORKED AROUND THE CLOCK TO
REGISTER BLACK VOTERS THROUGHOUT THE
SOUTH AND TO SHINE A SPOTLIGHT ON
BIGOTRY WHEREVER IT LIVED.

Voting is the foundation stone for political action.[1]

⸺◦⸺

Any real change in the status quo depends on continued creative action.[2]

⸺◦⸺

We can never be satisfied as long as a Negro in Mississippi cannot vote and a Negro in New York believes he has nothing for which to vote.[3]

⸺◦⸺

So long as I do not firmly and irrevocably possess the right to vote, I do not possess myself.[4]

Even where the polls are open to all, Negroes have shown themselves too slow to exercise their voting privileges.[5]

THE PEOPLE IN THIS PART OF THE WORLD WOULD DO WELL TO LISTEN TO DR. MARTIN LUTHER KING JR. AND GIVE HIM WHAT HE'S ASKING FOR, AND GIVE IT TO HIM FAST, BEFORE SOME OTHER FACTIONS COME ALONG AND TRY TO DO IT ANOTHER WAY.[6]

—*Malcolm X*

PRAYER PILGRIMAGE

IN MAY 1957 KING MADE HIS MARK ON THE NATIONAL STAGE BY ISSUING AN URGENT PLEA FOR VOTING RIGHTS REFORMS THROUGHOUT AMERICA. THE FORUM FOR THE SPEECH WAS THE PRAYER PILGRIMAGE FOR FREEDOM IN WASHINGTON D.C. IT WAS A STIRRING SPEECH AND A TURNING POINT IN KING'S CAREER AS A CIVIL RIGHTS LEADER.

The essence of man is found in freedom.[1]

The denial of this sacred right is a tragic betrayal of the highest mandates of our democratic tradition.[2]

Give us the ballot, and we will fill our legislative halls with men of goodwill and send to the sacred halls of Congress men who will not sign "a Southern Manifesto" because of their devotion to the manifesto of justice.[3]

In the past, apathy was a moral failure. Today it is a form of moral and political suicide.[4]

If America is to remain a first-class nation, it cannot have a second-class citizenship.[5]

Our most urgent request to the President of the United States and every member of Congress is to give us the right to vote. Give us the ballot and we will no longer have to worry the federal government about our basic rights.[6]

A CLOSE CALL

THE 1968 ASSASSINATION WAS NOT THE FIRST ATTEMPT ON KING'S LIFE. WHILE ON A TOUR TO PROMOTE HIS FIRST BOOK, *STRIDE TOWARD FREEDOM*, KING WAS ATTACKED BY A MENTALLY ILL WOMAN IN A DEPARTMENT STORE IN HARLEM, NEW YORK. THE WOMAN STABBED KING IN THE CHEST WITH A LETTER OPENER. WHILE RECUPERATING IN THE HOSPITAL, KING WAS INUNDATED WITH CARDS AND LETTERS, FEW MORE TOUCHING THAN THE ONE HE RECEIVED FROM ONE LITTLE GIRL:

DEAR DR. KING:
I AM A NINTH-GRADE STUDENT AT THE
WHITE PLAINS HIGH SCHOOL. WHILE IT
SHOULD NOT MATTER, I WOULD LIKE TO
MENTION THAT I AM A WHITE GIRL. I
READ IN THE PAPER OF YOUR MISFOR-
TUNE, AND OF YOUR SUFFERING. AND I
READ THAT IF YOU HAD SNEEZED, YOU
WOULD HAVE DIED. AND I'M SIMPLY
WRITING YOU TO SAY THAT I'M SO
HAPPY THAT YOU DIDN'T SNEEZE.[1]

PERSEVERANCE

KING'S MISSION WAS FULL OF OBSTACLES AND SOMETIMES HIS TACTICS FAILED. IN 1961 A MARCH TO ALBANY, GEORGIA, PROVED AN ABYSMAL FAILURE AFTER KING FAILED TO PROPERLY ORGANIZE HIS MARCHERS, AND HE FAILED TO ATTRACT ANY NATIONAL MEDIA ATTENTION TO HIS CAUSE. THE POLICE CHIEF IN ALBANY, LAURIE PRITCHETT, EVEN BOWED HIS HEAD WHEN KING LED THE PROTESTERS IN PRAYER. THE MISTAKES OF ALBANY WOULD NOT BE REPEATED. THROUGH PERSISTENCE AND A CONSTANT PENCHANT FOR LEARNING FROM HIS MISTAKES, KING BECAME A MASTER AT THE ART OF CIVIL DISOBEDIENCE.

We will err and falter as we climb the unfamiliar slopes of steep mountains, but there is no alternative, well-trod, level path.[1]

Our consolation is that no one can know the true taste of victory if he has never swallowed defeat.[2]

The oppressed must never allow the conscience of the oppressor to slumber.[3]

To accept injustice or segregation passively is to say to the oppressor that his actions are morally right.[4]

The first step toward eliminating any moral weakness is to concentrate on the higher virtue of calmness. You expel a lower vice by concentrating on a higher virtue.[5]

THE PEOPLE MADE DR. KING GREAT. HE ARTICULATES THE LONGINGS, THE HOPES, THE ASPIRATIONS OF HIS PEOPLE IN A MOST EARNEST AND PROFOUND MANNER. HE IS A HUMBLE MAN, DOWN TO EARTH, HONEST. HE HAS PROVED HIS COMMITMENT TO JUDEO-CHRISTIAN IDEALS. HE SEEKS TO SAVE THE NATION AND ITS SOUL.[6]

—*Rev. Ralph Abernathy*

FEW CAN EXPLAIN THE EXTRAORDINARY KING MYSTIQUE. YET HE HAS AN INDESCRIBABLE CAPACITY FOR EMPATHY THAT IS THE TOUCHSTONE OF LEADERSHIP. BY DEED AND PREACHMENT HE HAS STIRRED IN HIS PEOPLE A CHRISTIAN FORBEARANCE THAT NOURISHES HOPE AND SMOTHERS INJUSTICE.[7]

—Time *article in which King was named the magazine's 1964 Man of the Year*

MY OBJECTIVITY WENT OUT THE WINDOW WHEN I SAW THE PICTURE OF THOSE COPS SITTING ON THAT WOMAN AND HOLDING HER DOWN BY THE THROAT.[8]

—*Roy Wilkins, then head of the NAACP*

BIRMINGHAM

KING FORMED STRONG ALLIANCES TO ATTACK SEGREGATION AT ITS CORE. FORTUNATELY, THE CORE OF THE SEGREGATIONIST SOUTH WAS EASILY FOUND. IT WAS BIRMINGHAM, ALABAMA, WHERE OPPRESSION OF MINORITIES WAS FLAGRANT, AND WHITE RESIDENTS AND LEADERS WERE UNAPOLOGETIC FOR THEIR SEGREGATIONIST VIEWS. KING AND HIS FELLOW SCLC MEMBERS LAUNCHED A BOYCOTT OF DOWNTOWN BIRMINGHAM BUSINESSES, AND THEY ORGANIZED A MARCH FOR FREEDOM IN THE CITY. A COURT INJUNCTION WAS SOUGHT BARRING KING FROM MARCHING. THE ORDER WAS ISSUED, AND KING PROMPTLY IGNORED IT. ON APRIL 12, 1961, KING AND HIS FRIEND RALPH DAVID ABERNATHY DEFIED THE

COURT ORDER AND WERE ARRESTED BY BIRMINGHAM POLICE CHIEF EUGENE "BULL" CONNOR. THE TWO MEN WERE THROWN INTO SOLITARY CONFINEMENT.

FROM THAT JAIL CELL, KING WROTE HIS HISTORIC "LETTER FROM A BIRMINGHAM JAIL." SCRIBBLED IN THE MARGINS OF OLD NEWSPAPERS AND IN THE CORNERS OF A WORN-OUT LEGAL PAD, THE LETTER WAS ONE OF THE MOST MOVING AND THOUGHT-PROVOKING WORKS KING EVER PRODUCED.

My Dear Fellow Clergymen:
. . . I am in Birmingham because injustice is here. . . . Just as the Apostle Paul left his village of Tarsus and carried the gospel of Jesus Christ to the far corners of the Greco-Roman world, so am I compelled to carry the gospel of freedom beyond my own hometown.[1]

The absence of justice and progress in Birmingham demands that we make a moral witness to give our community a chance to survive.[2]

———

We will reach the goal of freedom in Birmingham and all over the nation, because the goal of America is freedom.[3]

———

If the inexpressible cruelties of slavery could not stop us, the opposition we now face will surely fail.[4]

———

We will win our freedom because the sacred heritage of our nation and the eternal will of God are embodied in our echoing demands.[5]

———

Injustice anywhere is a threat to justice everywhere.[6]

This 1957 photo shows King at a conference of Southern African-American leaders studying bus integration. Rev. Fred L. Shuttlesworth, on King's right, was one of those in attendance. (AP/Wide World photo)

Freedom is never voluntarily given by the oppressor; it must be demanded by the oppressed.[7]

Sometimes a law is just on its face and unjust in its application.[8]

Together we must learn to live as brothers, or together we will be forced to perish as fools.[9]

Our ultimate goal is integration, which is genuine intergroup and interpersonal living. Only through nonviolence can this goal be attained, for the aftermath of nonviolence is reconciliation and the creation of the beloved community.[10]

One of the great liabilities of history is that all too many people fail to remain awake through periods of social change.[11]

⎯⎯⎯

There comes a time when the cup of endurance runs over, and men are no longer willing to be plunged into an abyss of injustice where they experience the blackness of corroding despair.[12]

⎯⎯⎯

Oppressed people cannot remain oppressed forever.[13]

⎯⎯⎯

History is ultimately guided by spirit, not matter.[14]

⎯⎯⎯

On the one hand, integration is true intergroup, interpersonal living. On the other hand, it is the mutual sharing of power.[15]

⎯⎯⎯

Laws only declare rights; they do not deliver them. The oppressed must take hold of laws and transform them into effective mandates.[16]

⸺∿⸺

When a people are mired in oppression, they realize deliverance only when they have accumulated the power to enforce change.[17]

⸺∿⸺

CHILDREN'S CRUSADE

AS THE PROTESTS INCREASED AND THE CIVIL RIGHTS MOVEMENT GAINED MOMENTUM, KING ORGANIZED PROTESTS INVOLVING BIRMINGHAM'S BLACK SCHOOL CHILDREN. ON MAY 2, 1963, HUNDREDS OF CHILDREN FLOODED THE STREETS OF THE CITY SINGING "WE SHALL OVERCOME." BULL CONNOR ORDERED BIRMINGHAM POLICE TO BREAK UP THE MARCH USING FIRE HOSES AND BITING POLICE DOGS. THE HORRIFIC SCENES WERE BROADCAST ALL OVER THE NATION.

THREE DAYS LATER ANOTHER GROUP OF MARCHERS FILED TOWARD POLICE BARRICADES. CONNOR AGAIN ORDERED THE GROUP TO DISBURSE. WHEN THEY REFUSED, HE ORDERED THE FIRE HOSES TO BE TURNED ON. BUT THIS TIME THE POLICE REFUSED THE ORDER. THE MARCHERS PROCEEDED WITHOUT INCIDENT.

Our children must be taught to stand tall with their heads proudly lifted.[1]

Doors of opportunity are gradually opening now that were not open to our mothers and fathers. The great challenge is to prepare ourselves to enter these doors as they open.[2]

A hundred times I have been asked why we have allowed children to march in demonstrations, to freeze and suffer in jails, to be exposed to bullets and dynamite. . . . The answer is simple. Our children and our families are maimed a little every day of our lives. If we can end an incessant torture by a single climactic confrontation, the risks are acceptable.[3]

We were inspired with the desire to give to our young a true sense of their own stake in freedom and justice.[4]

These teenagers had that marvelous humor that arms the unarmed in the face of danger.[5]

We are moving up a mighty highway toward the city of Freedom.[6]

⸻

Massive civil disobedience is a strategy for social change which is at least as forceful as an ambulance with its siren on full.[7]

⸻

Somewhere along the way every child must be trained into the obligations of cooperative living. He must be made aware that he is a member of a group and that group life implies duties and restraints. Social life is possible only if there exists a balance between liberty and discipline.[8]

⸻

We found them eager
to belong, hungry for
participation in a
significant social effort.[9]

KING'S DREAM

ON AUGUST 28, 1963, KING LED A GROUP OF PROTESTERS TO WASHINGTON, D.C. ON THE STEPS OF THE LINCOLN MEMORIAL. IN FRONT OF A HALF MILLION CHEERING SUPPORTERS, KING MADE THE MOST ROUSING AND INSPIRATIONAL SPEECH OF HIS LIFE. FOR MANY IN THE NORTHEAST, THE MIDWEST, AND THE WEST COAST, IT WAS THE FIRST KING SPEECH THEY HAD HEARD. THE NATION AND THE WORLD WOKE UP TO THE CIVIL RIGHTS MOVEMENT THAT WARM SUMMER DAY IN WASHINGTON.

ALL THIS HASN'T CHANGED ANY VOTES ON THE CIVIL-RIGHTS BILL, BUT IT'S A GOOD THING FOR WASHINGTON AND THE NATION AND THE WORLD.[1]

—*Hubert H. Humphrey, senator*

I have a dream that one day this nation will rise up and live out the true meaning of its creed: "We hold these truths to be self-evident, that all men are created equal."[2]

When the architects of our republic wrote the magnificent words of the Constitution and the Declaration of Independence, they were signing a promissory note to which every American was to fall heir.[3]

WHEN KING FINISHED, GROWN MEN AND WOMEN STOOD IN THE SHADOW OF THE LEAVES AND WEPT UNCONTROLLABLY. KING'S SPEECH HAD AN IMPACT ON ITS AGE NOT UNLIKE THE TOTALLY DIFFERENT SPEECH OF BOOKER T. WASHINGTON SIXTY-EIGHT YEARS BEFORE. MAJOR NORTHERN PAPERS AND PERIODICALS QUOTED IT EXTENSIVELY, AND MANY ADDED EDITORIALLY THAT IT WAS "A MASTERPIECE." EVEN MORE IMPORTANT, KING'S WORDS WERE CARRIED VIA ELECTRONIC DEVICES TO MILLIONS MORE IN AMERICA, AFRICA, ASIA, AND EUROPE.[4]

—*Lerone Bennett Jr., author,* What Manner of Man: A Biography of Martin Luther King Jr.

I SEE AN AMERICA IN WHICH MARTIN LUTHER KING'S DREAM IS OUR NATIONAL DREAM.[5]

—*Jimmy Carter*

KING OFFERED A DREAM. THE CROWD ANSWERED BACK WITH APPLAUSE. KING RESPONDED WITH A NEW DREAM. IT WAS NO LONGER JUST CIVIL RIGHTS, IT WAS CIVIL RELIGION—THE NATION'S DESTINY AS THE ACCOMPLISHMENT OF GOD'S WILL.[6]

—*Nicolaus Mills, author*

EACH TIME THE DREAM WAS A PROMISE OUT OF OUR ANCIENT ARTICLES OF FAITH: PHRASES FROM THE CONSTITUTION, LINES FROM THE GREAT ANTHEM OF THE NATION, GUARANTEES FROM THE BILL OF RIGHTS, ALL ENDING WITH THE VISION THAT THEY MIGHT ONE DAY ALL COME TRUE.[7]

—*James Reston*, New York Times *columnist*

THAT DAY, FOR A MOMENT, IT ALMOST SEEMED THAT WE STOOD ON A HEIGHT AND COULD SEE OUR INHERITANCE. PERHAPS WE COULD MAKE THE KINGDOM REAL; PERHAPS THE BELOVED COMMUNITY WOULD NOT FOREVER REMAIN THAT DREAM ONE DREAMED IN AGONY.[8]

—*James Baldwin, author*

We are all in this together: ministers, professional people, and the masses.[9]

NOBEL PEACE PRIZE

IN 1964 PRESIDENT JOHNSON SIGNED THE CIVIL RIGHTS ACT INTO LAW. KING WAS ALSO NAMED *TIME* MAGAZINE'S MAN OF THE YEAR THAT JANUARY, AND LATER THAT YEAR, AT THE AGE OF THIRTY-FIVE, HE BECAME THE YOUNGEST MAN IN HISTORY TO WIN THE NOBEL PEACE PRIZE. UPON ACCEPTING THE AWARD IN OSLO, NORWAY, KING DONATED THE $54,000 HE RECEIVED FOR WINNING THE PRIZE TO THE CIVIL RIGHTS MOVEMENT.

I accept this award on behalf of a civil rights movement which is moving with determination and a majestic scorn for risk and danger to establish a reign of freedom and a rule of justice.[1]

I cannot forget that the Nobel Prize for Peace was also a commission—a commission to work harder than I had ever worked before for the brotherhood of man. This is a calling which takes me beyond national allegiances.[2]

I accept this award today with an abiding faith in America and an audacious faith in the future of mankind.[3]

Even amid today's mortar bursts and whining bullets, there is still hope for a brighter tomorrow.[4]

Nonviolence is not sterile passivity but a powerful moral force which makes for social transformation.[5]

The beauty of genuine brotherhood and peace is more precious than diamonds, or silver or gold.[6]

King holds a newspaper describing Los Angeles rioting in August
1965 as he speaks out against the West Coast violence while en
route to a speaking engagement. (AP/Wide World photo)

SELMA

WITH ONLY 1 PERCENT OF THE BLACK POP-
ULATION REGISTERED TO VOTE, SELMA,
ALABAMA, BECAME THE FOCUS OF KING'S
NONVIOLENT PROTESTS. BUT THE
PROTESTS IN SELMA WERE ANYTHING BUT
NONVIOLENT. EVEN THOUGH THE BLACK
MARCHERS, LED BY JOHN LEWIS,
REMAINED PEACEFUL, LAW-ENFORCEMENT
OFFICERS BRUTALIZED THE CITIZENRY.
HUNDREDS WERE ARRESTED—KING AMONG
THEM—WHILE OTHERS WERE BEATEN AND
SHOT. JAMIE LEE JACKSON DIED FROM A
BULLET FIRED BY AN ALABAMA STATE
TROOPER. JACKSON'S CRIME HAD BEEN TO
TRY TO PROTECT HIS MOTHER AND GRAND-
FATHER FROM THE ONSLAUGHT. JAMES
REEB, A WHITE MINISTER, WAS BEATEN TO
DEATH WHILE ANOTHER WHITE VOLUN-
TEER, VIOLA LIUZZO, WAS SHOT TO DEATH
WHILE DRIVING PROTESTERS TO SELMA.

BY MARCH 1965 THE VIOLENCE IN SELMA REACHED EVEN GREATER LEVELS. DURING A MARCH BY PROTESTERS FROM SELMA TO THE STATE CAPITAL TO PROTEST THE VIOLENCE ADMINISTERED BY LAW-ENFORCEMENT OFFICERS, STATE TROOPERS ATTACKED THE MARCHERS ON THE EDMUND PETTUS BRIDGE, BRUTALLY BEATING SENIOR CITIZENS WITH CLUBS. THE SCENE SHOCKED AND OUTRAGED THE NATION AND BECAME KNOWN AROUND THE WORLD AS BLOODY SUNDAY. TWO WEEKS LATER KING LED A TELEVISED MARCH OF HUNDREDS OF CELEBRITIES, POLITICIANS, AND CLERGY ALONG THE SAME ROUTE. ON THE STEPS OF THE CAPITOL BUILDING IN MONTGOMERY, KING DELIVERED ANOTHER STIRRING SPEECH. HIS WORDS PROMPTED CONGRESS TO PASS THE VOTING RIGHTS ACT ON AUGUST 6, 1965.

There is nothing more tragic in all this world than to know right and not do it.[1]

The end we seek is a society at peace with itself, a society that can live with its conscience.[2]

Today I want to tell the city of Selma, today I want to say to the state of Alabama, today I want to say to the people of America and the nations of the world, that we are not about to turn around. We are on the move now.[3]

WAR AND PEACE

KING WAS CONSISTENT IN HIS NONVIO-
LENT VIEWS. HE TOOK AN UNPOPULAR
STAND AND LOST A LOT OF POLITICAL SUP-
PORT BY SPEAKING OUT AGAINST THE
VIETNAM WAR TO THE CHAGRIN OF PRESI-
DENT LYNDON JOHNSON. BUT THERE WAS
NO OTHER WAY. TO DO OTHERWISE
WOULD HAVE GONE AGAINST EVERYTHING
KING BELIEVED IN.

We were taking the black young men who had been crip-
pled by our society and sending them eight thousand miles
away to guarantee liberties in Southeast Asia which they
had not found in southwest Georgia and East Harlem.[1]

The promises of the Great Society have been shot down on the battlefields of Vietnam. The bombs in Vietnam explode at home; they destroy the hopes and possibilities for a decent America. I am disappointed with our failure to deal positively and forthrightly with the triple evils of racism, extreme materialism, and militarism.[2]

If we don't have goodwill toward men in this world, we will destroy ourselves by the misuse of our own instruments and our own power.[3]

Many men cry, "Peace! Peace!" but they refuse to do the things that make for peace.[4]

It may be necessary to engage in civil disobedience to further arouse the conscience of a nation.[5]

—*King explaining his public opposition to the Vietnam War*

The war in Vietnam is but a symptom of a far-deeper malady within the American spirit.[6]

⸺⟨⟩⸺

If America's soul becomes totally poisoned, part of the autopsy must read Vietnam. It can never be saved so long as it destroys the hopes of men the world over.[7]

⸺⟨⟩⸺

Conflicts are never resolved without trustful give-and-take on both sides.[8]

⸺⟨⟩⸺

Mankind must put an end to war, or war will put an end to mankind.[9]

⸺⟨⟩⸺

Our government must depend more on its moral power than on its military power.[10]

⸺⟨⟩⸺

Our scientific power has outrun our spiritual power. We have guided missiles and misguided man.[11]

We say that war is a consequence of hate, but close scrutiny reveals this sequence: First fear, then hate, then war, and finally deeper hatred.[12]

I still believe that one day mankind will bow before the altars of God and be crowned triumphant over war and bloodshed, and nonviolent redemptive goodwill will proclaim the rule of the land.[13]

KING'S INFLUENCE

THE CHARISMATIC KING EMBODIED MANY OF THE CHARACTERISTICS TYPICAL OF GREAT LEADERS THAT CAME BEFORE HIM. WHEN HIS FOLLOWERS SANG THE MOVEMENT'S ANTHEM, "WE SHALL OVERCOME," THEY DID SO KNOWING THAT THEIR LEADER HAD A SPIRITUAL COMPASS TO MAKE THAT A REALITY. KING WAS COURAGEOUS, COMPASSIONATE, AND DEEPLY COMMITTED TO THE CIVIL RIGHTS MOVEMENT. HIS PERSUASIVE STYLE WAS REMARKABLE. KING COULD CALM AN ANGRY CROWD BY MERELY WAVING HIS HAND. AND HE COULD ENCOURAGE AND INSPIRE PROTESTERS TO MARCH NONVIOLENTLY FOR FREEDOM IN THE MIDST OF GRAVE DANGER.

PEOPLE LOVED KING . . . I'VE SEEN PEOPLE IN THE SOUTH
CLIMB OVER EACH OTHER JUST TO SAY, "I TOUCHED HIM! I
TOUCHED HIM!" I'M EVEN TALKING ABOUT THE YOUNG.[1]

—Stokely Carmichael, Black Power advocate

MARTIN HAD THE ABILITY TO MAKE US FEEL AS IF WE WERE
MORE THAN OUR DAILY SELVES, MORE THAN WE HAD BEEN—
A PART OF A BEAUTIFUL AND GLORIOUS VISION THAT WAS
ENABLING US TO TRANSCEND OURSELVES. IT WAS A MAR-
VELOUS QUALITY HE HAD, NOT EVER FULLY CAPTURED ON
THE PRINTED PAGE OR IN RECORDINGS, TO LIFT THE PEOPLE
TO ANOTHER PLACE SO THAT THEY COULD ALMOST FEEL
THEMSELVES MOVING.[2]

—Andrew Young

HE WAS ALWAYS THE EMBODIMENT OF THE KIND OF COURAGE
THAT WAS REQUIRED IF THE CIVIL RIGHTS MOVEMENT WAS
TO SUCCEED. HAD HE BEEN A COWARD RATHER THAN A
TRULY BRAVE MAN, THEN NONE OF THE REST OF US WOULD
HAVE FOLLOWED HIM, AND WE MIGHT STILL BE RIDING IN THE
BACK OF BUSES AND EATING IN SEGREGATED RESTAURANTS.[3]

—Rev. Ralph David Abernathy

(KING) EMERGED FROM THE PRAYER PILGRIMAGE TO WASHINGTON AS THE NUMBER-ONE LEADER OF SIXTEEN MILLION NEGROES IN THE UNITED STATES . . . AT THIS POINT IN HIS CAREER, THE PEOPLE WILL FOLLOW HIM ANYWHERE.[4]

—*James L. Hicks, editor,* New York Amsterdam News

PROBABLY THE GREATEST HUMAN BEING IN THE UNITED STATES TODAY.[5]

—*Adam Clayton Powell, congressman*

IN MY BOOK HE'S THE BEST AND FRESHEST THING THAT EVER HAPPENED IN AMERICA.[6]

—*Glenn Smiley, the Fellowship of Reconciliation*

HE (KING) WAS CONSIDERED, AT THE TIME, THE MOST RADICAL OF ALL AFRICAN-AMERICAN VOICES ON THE SCENE.[7]

—*Rev. Samuel B. McKinney, Morehouse College friend*

NONVIOLENCE

KING'S EXPOSURE AT A YOUNG AGE TO THE PACIFIST TEACHINGS OF GANDHI TOOK ROOT IN HIM AND DEFINED HIS PHILOSOPHY IN RALLYING BLACKS TO THE BURGEONING CIVIL RIGHTS MOVEMENT. NOT ALL BLACK LEADERS IN KING'S GENERATION WERE SOLD OUT TO HIS INSISTENCE THAT NONVIOLENCE BE THE PREFERRED MEANS TO AN END, BUT HE WAS PERSUASIVE IN ESTABLISHING AT LEAST A CONSENSUS, EVEN IF THE SUPPORT WASN'T UNANIMOUS. KING UNDERSTOOD THAT A NONVIOLENT CHALLENGE OF THE LAW AND OCCASIONAL JAIL TIME DID MORE TO INFLUENCE EVENTUAL POSITIVE CHANGE THAN DID THE VIOLENT SHEDDING OF BLOOD. KING MIGHT HAVE REASONED IT BETTER TO BE A LIVE MARTYR THAN A DEAD MARTYR BECAUSE THERE ALWAYS WAS MORE WORK TO BE DONE.

THE GOVERNMENT OF THE DAY HAS PASSED A LAW WHICH IS APPLICABLE TO ME. I DO NOT LIKE IT. IF BY USING VIOLENCE I FORCE THE GOVERNMENT TO REPEAL THE LAW, I AM EMPLOYING WHAT MAY BE CALLED BODY-FORCE. IF I DO NOT OBEY THE LAW AND ACCEPT THE PENALTY FOR THE BREACH, I USE SOUL-FORCE. IT INVOLVES SACRIFICE OF SELF.[1]

—*Gandhi*

Nonviolent resistance is not a method for cowards; it does resist. If one uses this method because he is afraid or merely because he lacks the instruments of violence, he is not truly nonviolent.[2]

—⊶∘⊷—

The alternative to violence is nonviolent resistance.[3]

—⊶∘⊷—

Nonviolent resistance is a willingness to accept suffering without retaliation, to accept blows from the opponent without striking back.[4]

—⊶∘⊷—

To ignore evil is to become an accomplice to it.[5]

—⊶∘⊷—

Appeal to the sense of morality and decency of the people on the other side of the negotiating table.[6]

———

The nonviolent resister is just as strongly opposed to the evil against which he protests as is the person who uses violence.[7]

———

Nonviolence is a way of humility and self-restraint.[8]

———

The believer in nonviolence has deep faith in the future. This faith is another reason why the nonviolent resister can accept suffering without retaliation.[9]

———

OH, GOD, WHEN IS THIS VIOLENCE GOING TO STOP?[10]

—*Bobby Kennedy's immediate reaction upon being told of King's assassination*

At the center of nonviolence stands the principle of love.[11]

Nonviolence provides a healthy way to deal with understandable anger.[12]

Nonviolence does not seek to defeat or humiliate the opponent, but to win his friendship and understanding.[13]

The reason you should not follow the old eye-for-an-eye philosophy is that it ends up leaving everybody blind.[14]

Nonviolent direct action will continue to be a significant source of power until it is made irrelevant by the presence of justice.[15]

⟶⟵

Through violence you may murder a murderer, but you can't murder murder. Through violence you may murder a liar, but you can't establish truth. Through violence you may murder a hater, but you can't murder hate.[16]

⟶⟵

If we are to have peace in the world, men and nations must embrace the nonviolent affirmation that ends and means must cohere.[17]

⟶⟵

The nonviolent resister not only refuses to shoot his opponent, but he also refuses to hate him.[18]

⟶⟵

Above all, our experience has shown that social change can take place without violence.[19]

⟶⟵

King answers questions at a September 1962 news conference in Birmingham during a Southern Christian Leadership Conference convention. (AP/Wide World photo)

INSPIRATION

> KING EPITOMIZED HOPE FOR BLACK AMERI-
> CANS AS WELL AS MANY OF HIS WHITE
> BRETHREN WHO SAW HIM AS SOMEONE WHO
> IDENTIFIED WITH ALL OPPRESSED PEOPLE.
> HE SAW THE GLASS AS HALF FULL AND HAD
> AN AMAZING KNACK FOR INSPIRING PEOPLE,
> ESPECIALLY AT TIMES WHEN THEY COULD
> HAVE SUCCUMBED, RUDDERLESS, TO SOR-
> ROW AND DESPAIR.

One day our society will come to respect the sanitation worker if it is to survive, for the person who picks up our garbage is in the final analysis as significant as the physician, for if he doesn't do his job, diseases are rampant. All labor has dignity.[1]

If you lose hope, somehow you lose that vitality that keeps life moving, you lose that courage to be, that quality that helps you to go on in spite of all.[2]

We must accept infinite disappointment, but we must never lose infinite hope.[3]

Every man must be respected because God loves him.[4]

Every act of injustice mars and defaces the image of God in man.[5]

All labor that uplifts humanity has dignity and worth and should be pursued with respect for excellence.[6]

Only through an inner spiritual transformation do we gain the strength to fight vigorously the evils of the world in a humble and loving spirit.[7]

We are inevitably our brother's keeper because we are our brother's brother. Whatever affects one directly affects all indirectly.[8]

Nothing worthwhile is gained without sacrifice.[9]

Never forget that freedom is not something that is voluntarily given by the oppressor. It is something that must be demanded by the oppressed.[10]

KING WAS NOT A MERE DREAMER, SETTING IDEALS FOR HUMANITY; HE WAS ALSO A DOER, A DRUM MAJOR FOR FREEDOM, JUSTICE, AND EQUALITY, LEADING AND INSPIRING MANY TO TAKE PRACTICAL STEPS TOWARD THE ATTAINMENT OF THOSE IDEALS.[11]

—*James A. Colaiaco, King biographer*

There comes a time when one must take a position that is neither safe, nor politic, nor popular, but he must do it because Conscience tells him it is right.[12]

Leadership is more inspiration than administration.[13]

People derive inspiration from their involvement.[14]

To produce change, people must be organized to work together in units of power.[15]

Human worth lies in relatedness to God.[16]

In our society it is murder, psychologically, to deprive a man of a job or an income.[17]

Man is a child of God, made in His image, and therefore must be respected as such.[18]

Every man must be respected because God loves him.[19]

An individual has value because he has value to God.[20]

Tie your vision to the human desire for a better tomorrow.[21]

CUISINE

KING LOVED FOOD AND APPRECIATED GOOD COOKING. HE HAD A HEALTHY APPETITE AND ENJOYED EATING DELICIOUS FOOD. KING OFTEN SPOKE ABOUT HIS SPECIAL RELATIONSHIP WITH HIS LOVING GRANDMOTHER AND HOW HE NEVER FORGOT THE GOOD BISCUITS SHE MADE FOR HIM. AFTER A LONG DAY ON THE ROAD CAMPAIGNING FOR FREEDOM, KING WOULD OFTEN HEAD TO HIS HOTEL ROOM TO MEET AND DINE WITH MEMBERS OF HIS STAFF. IT WAS IN THESE LATE-NIGHT MEETINGS THAT THE REAL DECISIONS AND DIRECTIONS OF THE CAMPAIGN WERE DETERMINED.

AND, OF COURSE, THERE WAS FOOD—MARTIN LOVED TO EAT
FRIED CHICKEN OR BARBECUED RIBS, OR BOTH.[1]

—*Andrew Young*

---

*Ralph David Abernathy recalls a time when King dined at his home
with him and his wife, Juanita:*

MARTIN LOVED FOOD AND WAS PARTICULARLY APPRECIATIVE
OF GOOD COOKS. HE WAS FOND OF JUANITA BECAUSE SHE
WAS BRIGHT AND QUICK-WITTED; BUT IT WAS ALSO HER
COOKING THAT MADE HER AMONG HIS FAVORITES. I REMEM-
BER ONE NIGHT IN MONTGOMERY WHEN SHE HAD SERVED
HOMEMADE ICE CREAM AND HE WAS ABOUT TO START ON
HIS SECOND BOWL. SUDDENLY, HE STOPPED WITH HIS SPOON
IN MIDAIR.

"JUANITA," HE SAID. "I BELIEVE WE CAN SOLVE THIS
WHOLE BOYCOTT PROBLEM IF WE CARRY A BOWL OF THIS ICE
CREAM OVER TO GEORGE WALLACE. I THINK I'LL TAKE IT
OVER RIGHT NOW." HE STARTED TO RISE, THEN SANK BACK
IN HIS CHAIR. "NO," HE SAID. "HE DOESN'T DESERVE IT. I'M
JUST GOING TO SIT HERE AND EAT IT MYSELF."[2]

A newsman interviews King, clutching a copy of a federal temporary restraining order, outside the police chief's office in Albany, Georgia, in 1962. (AP/Wide World photo)

KING'S ORATORY

KING WAS A POWERFUL, MAGNIFICENT SPEAKER. HE USED HIS ELOQUENT VOICE LIKE A FINE-TUNED INSTRUMENT, RAISING AND LOWERING IT AT JUST THE RIGHT MOMENTS TO DELIVER AN ELECTRIFYING MESSAGE THAT EVOKED EMOTION AS MUCH AS IT INSPIRED INTELLECT. KING, EVERY BIT A PREACHER'S SON, HAD A DISTINCTIVE STYLE HE STARTED HONING WHILE DELIVERING SPIRIT-FILLED SERMONS IN THE PULPIT OF HIS FATHER'S CHURCH. KING'S VOICE WAS PHENOMENAL AND CAPABLE OF MOVING, MOTIVATING, AND MESMERIZING ALL WHO HEARD IT.

WHEN HE SPOKE, YOU COULD HEAR A PIN DROP. THAT WAS HOW QUIET AND RECEPTIVE THE AUDIENCE WAS.[1]
—Yvonne Beatty, Mount Zion Baptist Church, Seattle

HE WAS THE RIGHT MAN AT THE RIGHT TIME AT THE RIGHT PLACE WITH THE RIGHT MESSAGE.[2]

—*Rev. Samuel B. McKinney, Morehouse College friend*

UNCONDITIONAL LOVE WAS WHAT HE HAD TO SAY, AND HE SAID IT SO VERY BEAUTIFULLY AND DEMONSTRATED IT SO WONDERFULLY.[3]

—*Rev. Dale Turner, Seattle*

I PERCEIVED IMMEDIATELY THAT THIS BOY WAS MATURE BEYOND HIS YEARS; THAT HE SPOKE AS A MAN WHO SHOULD HAVE HAD TEN MORE YEARS' EXPERIENCE THAN WAS POSSIBLE. HE HAD A BALANCE AND MATURITY THEN THAT WERE FAR BEYOND HIS YEARS AND A GRASP OF LIFE AND ITS PROBLEMS THAT EXCEEDED EVEN THAT.[4]

—*Benjamin E. Mays, Morehouse College president*

LOVE

KING LOVED ALL PEOPLE, INCLUDING HIS ENEMIES. BUT HE CAREFULLY QUALIFIED THAT BY SAYING THIS KIND OF LOVE WAS NOT TO BE CONFUSED WITH AFFECTION. THE LOVE HE ESPOUSED WAS ALIGNED WITH THE KIND OF LOVE JESUS CHRIST ASKED FROM HIS DISCIPLES AND FOLLOWERS, IN WHICH YOU RECOGNIZE AND RESPECT OTHERS AS CHILDREN OF GOD, ALL ELIGIBLE FOR ETERNAL REDEMPTION.

KING EXPLAINED THAT IN THE GREEK LANGUAGE THERE ARE THREE WORDS FOR LOVE: *EROS*, OR ROMANTIC LOVE; *PHILIA*, WHICH IS INTIMATE AFFECTION BETWEEN FRIENDS OR A MAN AND A WOMAN; AND *AGAPE*, DEFINED AS UNDERSTANDING, REDEEMING GOODWILL FOR ALL MEN. AGAPE WAS THE KIND OF LOVE THAT PROVIDED THE FOUNDATION FOR KING'S NONVIOLENCE DOCTRINE.

Along the way of life, someone must have sense enough and morality enough to cut off the chain of hate and evil.[1]

Love is a potent instrument for social and collective transformation.[2]

Take time to compose a letter or speak on the phone with people who disagree with you.[3]

We must develop and maintain the capacity to forgive.[4]

Hate scars the soul and distorts the personality.[5]

LOVE THE HELL OUT OF THEM, HE WOULD SAY. AND HE MEANT THAT LITERALLY. IF THERE IS HELL IN SOMEONE, IF THERE IS MEANNESS AND ANGER AND HATRED IN HIM, WE'VE GOT TO *LOVE* IT OUT.[6]

—*John Lewis*

You may give your goods to feed the poor, you may bestow great gifts to charity, and you may tower high in philanthropy, but if you have not love, your charity means nothing.[7]

Standing beside love is always justice.[8]

Love is one of the pivotal points of the Christian faith.[9]

Love is a transforming power that can lift a whole community to new horizons of fair play, goodwill, and justice.[10]

Love is unconditional.[11]

Justice at its best is love correcting everything that stands against love.[12]

Power without love is reckless and abusive, and love without power is sentimental and anemic.[13]

The hard-hearted person never truly loves.[14]

I am convinced that the universe is under the control of a loving purpose.[15]

Love is understanding, creative, redemptive goodwill toward all men.[16]

HUMOR

AS SERIOUS AND EVEN REGAL AS HE CAME ACROSS IN PUBLIC, KING ALSO HAD A LIGHTER SIDE. HE HAD A LIVELY SENSE OF HUMOR, WHICH HE SOMETIMES USED TO DIFFUSE INTENSE SITUATIONS. IT WAS A FUN-LOVING QUALITY THAT HELPED ROUND OUT THE WHOLE MAN.

In his book Stride Toward Freedom, *King recalls a humorous incident he shared with inmates at the Montgomery city jail after he was arrested during the bus boycott:*

They all gathered around to find out why I was there, and showed some surprise that the city had gone so far as to arrest me. Soon one man after another began talking to me about his reason for being in jail and asking if I could help him get out. After the third person had asked my help, I turned to the group and said: "Fellows, before I can assist in getting any of you out, I've got to get my ownself out." At this they laughed.[1]

Humor

In his book An Easy Burden, *Andrew Young remembers a light moment with King, when he, Ralph Abernathy, and other SCLC members registering blacks to vote in Mississippi stopped at a little country store for gas:*

WE HADN'T EATEN THE ENTIRE DAY. ON THE COUNTER WAS A TWO-GALLON JAR OF PICKLED PIGS' FEET. MARTIN AND RALPH AND OTHERS IN THE CARAVAN STARTED BUYING PIGS' FEET, ONE BY ONE. THEN MARTIN JUST SHRUGGED AND BOUGHT THE WHOLE JAR. THEY STOOD AROUND THIS LITTLE COUNTRY STORE IN THE MIDDLE OF MISSISSIPPI EATING PIGS' FEET LIKE THEY WERE GOING OUT OF STYLE. MARTIN TRIED UNSUCCESSFULLY TO GET ME TO EAT ONE. "COME ON, ANDY," HE TEASED, "YOU KNOW THEY EAT PIGS' FEET IN NEW ORLEANS!" AND HE AND RALPH HAD A GOOD LAUGH AT MY EXPENSE.[2]

HE ALWAYS HAD A PLAYFUL SENSE OF HUMOR AND LIKED PRACTICAL JOKES.[3]

—*Coretta Scott King*

MARTIN WAS FUN-LOVING, AND WHEN HE WAS OFFSTAGE YOU COULD USUALLY FIND HIM TELLING A JOKE OR TEASING SOMEBODY. HE HAD A PERFECT SENSE OF TIMING AND HE INSTINCTIVELY KNEW WHAT WAS FUNNY. SOME PEOPLE HAVE THAT GIFT AND SOME PEOPLE DON'T. HE HAD IT. I'M CON-VINCED THAT IF HE HAD WANTED TO BE A STANDUP COMIC HE COULD HAVE BEEN ALMOST AS FAMOUS IN THAT ROLE.[4]

—Ralph Abernathy

HE TEASED, HE COULD CRACK ON YOU, INSULT YOU UNTIL THE WHOLE ROOM WAS LAUGHING 'TIL THEY CRIED. BUT IT WAS NEVER IN ANGER, NEVER IN BITTERNESS, IT WAS ALWAYS IN FUN. MARTIN WOULD NEVER TEASE ANYONE HE DIDN'T LOVE.[5]

—Andrew Young

KING'S LAST DAY

STANDING ON THE BALCONY OF THE LOR-
RAINE MOTEL IN MEMPHIS, TENNESSEE, ON
APRIL 4, 1968, KING WAS SHOT TO DEATH
BY, ALLEGEDLY, WHITE SUPREMACIST
JAMES EARL RAY . KING WAS THIRTY-NINE
YEARS OLD. THE NIGHT BEFORE HE DIED,
KING SPOKE AT THE MASONIC TEMPLE IN
MEMPHIS. HIS WORDS, WHICH FOLLOW
BELOW, TURNED OUT TO BE A CHILLING
PROPHECY OF THE DAYS AHEAD.

I just want to do God's will. And He's allowed me to go
up to the Mountaintop and I've looked over. I've *seen*
the promised land. I may not get there with you, but I
want you to know tonight, that we as a people will get
to the promised land . . . I'm not fearing any man. Mine
eyes have *seen* the coming of the glory of the Lord.[1]

If you one day find me sprawled out dead, I do not want you to retaliate with a single act of violence.[2]

Death is inevitable . . . We need not fear it. The God who brought our whirling planet from primal vapor and has led the human pilgrimage for lo these many centuries can most assuredly lead us through death's dark night into the bright daybreak of eternal life.[3]

The fear of death, nonbeing, and nothingness, expressed in existential anxiety, may be cured only by a positive religious faith.[4]

Is someone here moving toward the twilight of life and fearful of that which we call death? Why be afraid? God is able.[5]

⸻

The thing that makes me happy is that I can hear a voice crying through the vista of time, saying, "It may not come today or it may not come tomorrow, but it is well that it is within thine heart. It's well that you are trying." You may not see it.[6]

—spoken in Memphis the day before he was assassinated

⸻

KING WAS WILLING TO CHALLENGE THE EVIL OF HATRED AND RACISM BY PUTTING HIS OWN LIFE ON THE LINE.[7]

—Rev. Samuel B. McKinney, Morehouse College friend

⸻

Our earthly life is a prelude to a glorious new awakening, and death is an open door that leads us into eternal life.[8]

A FINAL TRIBUTE

GO TO ANY CITY IN AMERICA AND YOU WILL
FIND A BUILDING, A STREET, A MONUMENT,
OR A PARK NAMED AFTER MARTIN LUTHER
KING, JR. HIS LEGACY HAS ENDURED AND
EVEN GROWN SINCE HIS DEATH. ON
NOVEMBER 2, 1983, PRESIDENT RONALD
REAGAN SIGNED A LAW PROCLAIMING A
NEW NATIONAL HOLIDAY TO BE CALLED
MARTIN LUTHER KING DAY IN OBSERVANCE
OF KING'S BIRTHDAY. IT IS OBSERVED
EVERY THIRD MONDAY IN JANUARY.

BEHOLD, HERE COMES THE DREAMER. LET US SLAY
HIM, AND WE SHALL SEE WHAT BECOMES OF HIS
DREAM.[1]

—plaque in the Memphis hotel room
where King was staying the day he was assassinated

TRULY GOD IS NO RESPECTER OF PERSONS. HOW STRANGE! GOD CALLED THE GRANDSON OF A SLAVE ON HIS FATHER'S SIDE AND SAID TO HIM: "MARTIN LUTHER, SPEAK TO AMERICA ABOUT WAR AND PEACE; ABOUT SOCIAL JUSTICE AND RACIAL DISCRIMINATION; ABOUT ITS OBLIGATIONS TO THE POOR; AND ABOUT NONVIOLENCE AS A WAY OF PERFECTING SOCIAL CHANGE IN THE WORLD OF BRUTALITY AND WAR."[2]

—Benjamin Mays, delivering King's eulogy

MARTIN LUTHER KING DEDICATED HIS LIFE TO LOVE AND TO JUSTICE FOR HIS FELLOW HUMAN BEINGS, AND HE DIED BECAUSE OF THAT EFFORT.[3]

—Bobby Kennedy, in a speech on April 4, 1968, just hours after King was assassinated

WHETHER OR NOT HISTORY IN THE FUTURE WILL PRODUCE ANOTHER SUCH LEADER REMAINS TO BE SEEN. I DOUBT IT. BECAUSE THE TIMES HAVE CHANGED. MARTIN WAS THE RIGHT MAN, WITH THE RIGHT TALENTS, AT THE RIGHT TIME.[4]

—Rev. Joseph Lowery, SCLC cofounder

HE IS SOMEONE WHO WE THINK WE KNOW. HE WAS THE NATION'S PREACHER AND OUR MOST PROMINENT MORAL PHILOSOPHER. HIS PHOTOGRAPH IS ON DISPLAY IN ELEMENTARY AND SECONDARY SCHOOLS ALL ACROSS AMERICA; AND IT'S DIFFICULT TO VISIT A MAJOR AMERICAN CITY AND NOT FIND A STREET OR A PUBLIC BUILDING NAMED AFTER HIM.[5]

—*Charles Johnson, author of* Dreamer, *a novel based on King's life*

AMERICANS LONG FOR SINGLE, HEROIC LEADERSHIP, THE LONE FIGURE DELIVERING SALVATION. KING BECAME THAT FIGURE, BUT HE CAME FROM A MOVEMENT THAT WAS GROUP-CENTERED, REPRESENTING DEMOCRACY AT ITS BEST.[6]

—*Julian Bond*

MARTIN HAD ALWAYS SAID THAT IN THE EVENT OF HIS DEATH—AND HE THOUGHT IT CERTAIN HE WOULD NOT LIVE OUT HIS DAYS TO OLD AGE—WE SHOULD CONTINUE ON, NOT PAUSING FOR ONE MINUTE. "IF YOU DO THIS," HE HAD TOLD US, "YOU'LL PROVE A MOVEMENT CAN'T BE KILLED BY KILLING THE LEADERS."[7]

—*Andrew Young*

AP/Wide World photo

HE WAS A GENIUS. I AM NOT TALKING ABOUT MY SON WHEN I SAY THAT; I'M TALKING ABOUT A WORLD CITIZEN. HE MOVED BEYOND US EARLY. HE DID NOT BELONG TO US, HE BELONGED TO THE WORLD.[8]

—*Rev. Martin Luther King Sr.*

BIBLIOGRAPHY

Abernathy, Ralph David, *And The Walls Came Tumbling Down*. New York: Harper and Row, 1989.

Adams, Russell, "The Legacy of Dr. Martin Luther King Jr.," *Black Collegian*, February 2001.

Altman, Susan, *The Encyclopedia of African-American Heritage*. New York: Facts On File, 1997.

Ayres, Alex, *The Wisdom of Martin Luther King Jr.* New York: The Penguin Group, 1993.

Bennett, Lerone Jr., *What Manner of Man: A Biography of Martin Luther King Jr.*, seventh revised ed. Chicago: Johnson Publishing Co., 1989.

Bourne, Peter G., *Jimmy Carter*. New York: A Lisa Drew Book/Scribner, 1997.

Carson, Clayborne, ed., *The Autobiography of Martin Luther King Jr.* New York: Warner Books, 1998.

Carson, Clayborne, and Peter Holloran, eds., *A Knock At Midnight*, Original Recordings of Reverend Martin Luther King Jr. New York: Time Warner Audio Books, 1998.

Carson, Clayborne, and Kris Shepard, *A Call To Conscience*. New York: Warner Books, 2001.

Carter, Jimmy, *A Government as Good as Its People*. New York: Simon and Schuster, 1977.

"Celebrating African American Independence Day," *The New Crisis*, May/June 2001. Baltimore, MD: The Crisis Publishing Company.

Colaiaco, James A., *Martin Luther King Jr.: Apostle of Militant Nonviolence*. New York: St. Martin's Press, 1993.

Cone, James H., *Martin & Malcolm & America*. Maryknoll, NY: Orbis Books, 1991.

David, Lester, and Irene David, *Bobby Kennedy: The Making of a Folk Hero*. New York: Dodd, Mead, and Company, 1986.

Deats, Richard, *Martin Luther King, Jr., Spirit-Led Prophet: A Biography*. New York: New City Press, 2000.

Erskine, Noel Leo, *King Among The Theologians*. Cleveland, OH: The Pilgrim Press, 1994.

Fairclough, Adam, *Martin Luther King Jr.* Athens, GA: University of Georgia Press, 1995.

Franklin, V. P., *Martin Luther King Jr.: Biography*. New York: Park Lane Press, 1998.

Free At Last! Free At Last! Told by Coretta Scott King from her book, *My Life with Martin Luther King Jr.*, Caedmon Records, New York.

Garrow, David J., *Bearing the Cross*. New York: William Morrow and Company, 1986.

Gates, Henry Louis, and Cornel West, *The African American Century*. New York: The Free Press, 2000.

Johnson, Charles, *Dreamer*. New York: Scribner, 1998.

King: The Photobiography of Martin Luther King Jr., introduction and essays by Charles Johnson. New York: Penguin Group, 2000.

King, Bernice A., *Hard Questions, Heart Answers*. New York: Broadway Books, 1997.

King, Coretta Scott, *My Life With Martin Luther King Jr.* Holt, Rinehart and Winston of Canada, 1969.

King, Coretta Scott, *The Words of Martin Luther King Jr.* New York: Newmarket Press, 1987.

King, Martin Luther Jr., *The Strength to Love*. Philadelphia: Fortress Press, 1981.

King, Martin Luther Jr., *Stride Toward Freedom*. New York: Harper & Row, 1986.

Bibliography

King, Martin Luther Jr., *The Trumpet of Conscience*. New York: Harper and Row, 1967.

King, Martin Luther Jr., *Where Do We Go From Here: Chaos or Community?* Boston: Beacon Press, 1968.

"King Speaks to the 21st Century," *Ebony*, January 2001.

Lewis, David L., *King: A Biography*. Champaign, IL: University of Illinois Press, 1978.

Lewis, John, with Michael D'Orso, *Walking with the Wind: A Memoir of the Movement*. New York: Simon and Schuster, 1998.

Lydon, Michael, *Ray Charles: Man and Music*. New York: Riverhead Books, 1998.

Martin Luther King Jr.: Apostle of Militant Nonviolence. New York: St. Martin's Press, 1993.

Martin Luther King Jr. Companion, The. New York: St. Martin's Press, 1993.

Miller, Keith D., *Voice of Deliverance: The Language of Martin Luther King, Jr. and Its Sources*. New York: The Free Press, 1992.

Oates, Stephen B., *Let the Trumpet Sound: A Life of Martin Luther King Jr.* New York: HarperCollins, 1982.

Phillips, Donald T., *Martin Luther King Jr. on Leadership*. New York: Warner Books, 1998.

Ray, James Earl, *Who Killed Martin Luther King?* Bethesda, MD: National Press Books, 1992.

Siebold, Thomas, ed., *Martin Luther King Jr.: People Who Made History*. San Diego, CA: Greenhaven Press, 2000.

Washington, James M., ed., *A Testament of Hope: The Essential Writings of Martin Luther King Jr.* New York: Harper and Row, 1986.

Young, Andrew, *An Easy Burden*. New York: HarperCollins, 1996.

NOTES

Segregation

1. King, Martin Luther Jr., *Stride Toward Freedom*. New York: Harper and Row, 1986, 20–21.

2. *Martin Luther King Jr. Companion, The*. New York: St. Martin's Press, 1993, 3.

3. Franklin, V. P., *Martin Luther King Jr.: Biography*. New York: Park Lane Press, 1998, 29.

4. *Martin Luther King Jr. Companion, The*. New York: St. Martin's Press, 1993, 9.

5. Ibid., 33.

6. Ibid.

7. Adams, Russell, "The Legacy of Dr. Martin Luther King Jr.," *Black Collegian*, February 2001, 88–89.

8. King, Martin Luther Jr., *Stride Toward Freedom*. New York: Harper and Row, 1986, 205.

9. King, Martin Luther Jr., *Where Do We Go From Here: Chaos Or Community?* Boston: Beacon Press, 1968, 97.

10. Ibid.

11. Bourne, Peter G., *Jimmy Carter*. New York: A Lisa Drew Book/Scribner, 1997, 325.

12. King, Martin Luther Jr., *Where Do We Go From Here: Chaos Or Community?* Boston: Beacon Press, 1968, 97.

13. Ibid., 100.

14. Ibid., 97.

15. *Martin Luther King Jr. Companion, The*. New York: St. Martin's Press, 1993, 48.

Faith

1. King, Martin Luther Jr., *The Strength to Love*. Philadelphia: Fortress Press, 1981, 84.

2. Ibid.
3. Erskine, Noel Leo, *King Among the Theologians*. Cleveland, OH: The Pilgrim Press, 1994, 9.
4. King, Martin Luther Jr., *The Strength to Love*. Philadelphia: Fortress Press, 1981, 19.
5. Ibid.
6. Ayres, Alex, ed., *The Wisdom of Martin Luther King Jr.* New York: Penguin Books USA, 1993, x.
7. Franklin, V. P., *Martin Luther King Jr.: Biography*. New York: Park Lane Press, 1998, 86.
8. Phillips, Donald T., *Martin Luther King Jr. on Leadership*. New York: Warner Books, 1998, 311.
9. King, Martin Luther Jr., *The Strength to Love*. Philadelphia: Fortress Press, 1981, 131.
10. Ibid., 134.
11. Franklin, V. P., *Martin Luther King Jr.: Biography*. New York: Park Lane Press, 1998, 17.
12. Erskine, Noel Leo, *King Among the Theologians*. Cleveland, OH: The Pilgrim Press, 1994, 143.
13. *Time*, January 3, 1964.
14. King, Martin Luther Jr., *The Strength to Love*. Philadelphia: Fortress Press, 1981, 153.
15. Carson, Clayborne, and Peter Holloran, eds., *A Knock at Midnight*. New York: Intellectual Properties Management, Inc., Time Warner Audio Books, 1998, 7.
16. Ibid., 10.
17. Ibid., 15.
18. Ibid., 18
19. Ibid., 30.
20. Ibid., 31
21. Ibid.
22. King, Martin Luther Jr., *The Strength to Love*. Philadelphia: Fortress Press, 1981, 153.

23. *Martin Luther King Jr. Companion, The*. New York: St. Martin's Press, 1993, 52.
24. "King Speaks to the 21st Century," *Ebony*, January 2001, 53–55.
25. *Martin Luther King Jr. Companion, The*. New York: St. Martin's Press, 1993, 52.
26. Ibid., 53.
27. King, Martin Luther Jr., *The Strength to Love*. Philadelphia: Fortress Press, 1981, 78.
28. "King Speaks to the 21st Century," *Ebony*, January 2001, 53–55.
29. Bourne, Peter G., *Jimmy Carter*. New York: A Lisa Drew Book/Scribner, 1997, 325.
30. "King Speaks to the 21st Century," *Ebony*, January 2001, 53–55.

Education
1. Ayres, Alex, ed., *The Wisdom of Martin Luther King Jr*. New York: Penguin Books USA, 1993, 243.
2. Phillips, Donald T., *Martin Luther King Jr. on Leadership*. New York: Warner Books, 1998, 216.
3. King, Martin Luther Jr., *Where Do We Go From Here: Chaos Or Community?* Boston: Beacon Press, 1968, 193.
4. Ibid., 194.
5. Ibid.
6. Ibid., 155.
7. Ibid.
8. Ibid., 194–195.
9. Ibid., 195.
10. Ibid., 193.
11. Phillips, Donald T., *Martin Luther King Jr. on Leadership*. New York: Warner Books, 1998, 86.
12. Bennett, Lerone Jr., *What Manner of Man: A Biography of Martin Luther King Jr*. Chicago: Johnson Publishing Co., 1976, 29.

Gandhi

1. King, Martin Luther Jr., *Where Do We Go From Here: Chaos Or Community?* Boston: Beacon Press, 1968, 44.
2. Carson, Clayborne, ed., *The Autobiography of Martin Luther King Jr.* New York: Warner Books, 1998, 24.
3. Ibid.
4. Ibid., 26.
5. King, Martin Luther Jr., *Stride Toward Freedom.* New York: Harper and Row, 1986, 85.
6. Ibid., 98.

Coretta

1. Carson, Clayborne, ed., *The Autobiography of Martin Luther King Jr.* New York: Warner Books, 1998, 34.
2. Ibid., 37.
3. Ibid.
4. *Martin Luther King Jr. Companion, The.* New York: St. Martin's Press, 1993, 97.

Civil Rights Movement

1. King, Martin Luther Jr., *Stride Toward Freedom.* New York: Harper and Row, 1986, 63.
2. Carter, Jimmy, *A Government as Good as Its People.* New York: Simon and Schuster, 1977, 26.
3. Mills, Judie, *Robert Kennedy.* Brookfield, CT: The Millbrook Press, 1998, 142.
4. Ibid., 143.
5. Carson, Clayborne, ed., *The Autobiography of Martin Luther King Jr.* New York: Warner Books, 1998, 60.
6. *Time,* January 3, 1964.
7. King, Martin Luther Jr., *Where Do We Go From Here: Chaos Or Community?* Boston: Beacon Press, 1968, 20.
8. *Martin Luther King Jr. Companion, The.* New York: St. Martin's Press, 1993, 13.

Notes

9. King, Martin Luther Jr., *Stride Toward Freedom*. New York: Harper and Row, 1986, 150.

10. Ibid., 223.

11. *Seattle Times*, November 9, 1996.

12. Lewis, John, with Michael D'Orso, *With the Wind: A Memoir of the Movement*. New York: Simon and Schuster, 1998, 208.

13. Colaiaco, James A., *Martin Luther King Jr.: Apostle of Militant Nonviolence*, excerpted from *The Civil Rights Reader*, Leon Friedman, ed. New York: St. Martin's Press, 1993, 69.

The SCLC

1. Washington, James M., ed., *A Testament of Hope, The Essential Writings of Martin Luther King Jr.* New York: Harper and Row, 1986, 183.

2. Ayres, Alex, ed., *The Wisdom of Martin Luther King Jr.* New York: Penguin Books USA, 1993, 230.

3. Ibid.

4. Phillips, Donald T., *Martin Luther King Jr. on Leadership*. New York: Warner Books, 1998, 135.

5. *Martin Luther King Jr. Companion, The*. New York: St. Martin's Press, 1993, 7.

6. Lewis, John, with Michael D'Orso, *Walking with the Wind: A Memoir of the Movement*. New York: Simon and Schuster, 1998, 313.

Prayer Pilgrimage

1. King, Martin Luther Jr., *Where Do We Go From Here: Chaos Or Community?* Boston: Beacon Press, 1968, 98.

2. Carson, Clayborne, and Kris Shepard, eds., *A Call to Conscience*. New York: Warner Books, 2001, 47.

3. Ibid., 48.

4. King, Martin Luther Jr., *Stride Toward Freedom*. New York: Harper and Row, 1986, 222.

5. Ibid., 197.

6. Carson, Clayborne, ed., *The Autobiography of Martin Luther King Jr.* New York: Warner Books, 1998, 108.

A Close Call

1. Carson, Clayborne, ed., *The Autobiography of Martin Luther King Jr.* New York: Warner Books, 1998, 118.

Perseverance

1. King, Martin Luther Jr., *Where Do We Go From Here: Chaos Or Community?* Boston: Beacon Press, 1968, 138.
2. Ibid.
3. *Martin Luther King Jr. Companion, The.* New York: St. Martin's Press, 1993, 49.
4. Ibid.
5. "King Speaks to the 21st Century," *Ebony*, January 2001, 53–55.
6. *Time*, January 3, 1964.
7. Ibid.
8. Ibid.

Birmingham

1. Carson, Clayborne, ed., *The Autobiography of Martin Luther King Jr.* New York: Warner Books, 1998, 188–189.
2. Colaiaco, James A., *Martin Luther King Jr.: Apostle of Militant Nonviolence.* New York: St. Martin's Press, 1993, 59.
3. Carson, Clayborne, ed., *The Autobiography of Martin Luther King Jr.* New York: Warner Books, 1998, 202.
4. Ibid.
5. Ibid.
6. Ibid., 189.
7. Ibid., 191.
8. Ibid., 194.
9. King, Martin Luther Jr., *Where Do We Go From Here: Chaos Or Community?* Boston: Beacon Press, 1968, 171.
10. King, Martin Luther Jr., *Stride Toward Freedom.* New York: Harper and Row, 1986, 220.

11. King, Martin Luther Jr., *Where Do We Go From Here: Chaos Or Community?* Boston: Beacon Press, 1968, 171.

12. Washington, James M., ed., *A Testament of Hope, The Essential Writings of Martin Luther King Jr.* New York: Harper and Row, 1986, 293.

13. Ibid., 297.

14. King, Martin Luther Jr., *Stride Toward Freedom.* New York: Harper and Row, 1986, 92.

15. King, Martin Luther Jr., *Where Do We Go From Here: Chaos Or Community?* Boston: Beacon Press, 1968, 62.

16. Ibid., 158.

17. Washington, James M., ed., *A Testament of Hope, The Essential Writings of Martin Luther King Jr.* New York: Harper and Row, 1986, 303.

Children's Crusade

1. King, Martin Luther Jr., *Where Do We Go From Here: Chaos Or Community?* Boston: Beacon Press, 1968, 123.

2. Ibid., 126.

3. King, Coretta Scott, *The Words of Martin Luther King Jr.* New York: Newmarket Press, 1987, 54.

4. Carson, Clayborne, ed., *The Autobiography of Martin Luther King Jr.* New York: Warner Books, 1998, 206.

5. Ibid., 208.

6. Ibid., 209.

7. King, Martin Luther Jr., *The Trumpet of Conscience.* New York: Harper & Row, 1967, 53.

8. "King Speaks to the 21st Century," *Ebony,* January 2001.

9. Carson, Clayborne, ed., *The Autobiography of Martin Luther King Jr.* New York: Warner Books, 1998, 206.

King's Dream

1. Colaiaco, James A., *Martin Luther King Jr.: Apostle of Militant Nonviolence.* New York: St. Martin's Press, 1993, 74.

2. Carson, Clayborne, and Kris Shepard, eds., *A Call to Conscience*. New York: Warner Books, 2001, 85.

3. Washington, James M., ed., *A Testament of Hope, The Essential Writings of Martin Luther King Jr*. New York: Harper and Row, 1986, 217.

4. Bennett, Lerone Jr., *What Manner of Man: A Biography of Martin Luther King Jr.*, seventh revised ed. Chicago: Johnson Publishing Co., 1989, 162–63.

5. Ayres, Alex, ed., *The Wisdom of Martin Luther King Jr*. New York: Penguin Books USA, 1993, ix.

6. Mills, Nicolaus, *Like a Holy Crusade: Mississippi 1964: The Turning of the Civil Rights Movement in America*. Chicago: Ivan R. Dee, 1992, 29–30.

7. Ibid., 30–31.

8. Colaiaco, James A., *Martin Luther King Jr.: Apostle of Militant Nonviolence*. New York: St. Martin's Press, 1993, 74.

9. Adams, Russell, "The Legacy of Dr. Martin Luther King Jr.," *Black Collegian*, February 2001, 88–89.

Nobel Peace Prize

1. Carson, Clayborne, and Kris Shepard, eds., *A Call to Conscience*. New York: Warner Books, 2001, 105.

2. Ayres, Alex, ed., *The Wisdom of Martin Luther King Jr*. New York: Penguin Books USA, 1993, 163.

3. Carson, Clayborne, eds., *The Autobiography of Martin Luther King Jr*. New York: Warner Books, 1998, 260.

4. Washington, James M., ed., *A Testament of Hope, The Essential Writings of Martin Luther King Jr*. New York: Harper and Row, 1986, 226.

5. Ibid., 225.

6. Ibid.

Selma

1. Oates, Stephen B., *Let the Trumpet Sound: A Life of Martin Luther King Jr*. New York: HarperCollins, 1982, 351.

2. Washington, James M., ed., *A Testament of Hope, The Essential Writings of Martin Luther King Jr.* New York: Harper and Row, 1986,, 230.

3. Carson, Clayborne, and Kris Shepard, ed., *A Call to Conscience.* New York: Warner Books, 2001, 125.

War and Peace

1. King, Martin Luther Jr., *The Trumpet of Conscience.* New York: Harper and Row, 1967, 23.

2. Young, Andrew, *An Easy Burden.* New York: HarperCollins, 1996, 429.

3. King, Martin Luther Jr., *The Trumpet of Conscience.* New York: Harper and Row, 1967, 67.

4. Colaiaco, James A., *Martin Luther King Jr.: Apostle of Militant Nonviolence,* excerpted from *New York Times,* April 4, 1967. New York: St. Martin's Press, 1993, 179.

5. King, Martin Luther Jr., *The Trumpet of Conscience.* New York: Harper and Row, 1967, 68.

6. Ibid., 32.

7. *Martin Luther King Jr. Companion, The.* New York: St. Martin's Press, 1993, 87.

8. Washington, James M., ed., *A Testament of Hope, The Essential Writings of Martin Luther King Jr.* New York: Harper and Row, 1986, 635.

9. Ibid., 276.

10. King, Martin Luther Jr., *Where Do We Go From Here: Chaos Or Community?* Boston: Beacon Press, 1968,133.

11. *Martin Luther King Jr. Companion, The.* New York: St. Martin's Press, 1993, 83.

12. Ibid.

13. King, Coretta Scott, *The Words of Martin Luther King Jr.* New York: Newmarket Press, 1987, 91.

King's Influence

1. Ayres, Alex, ed., *The Wisdom of Martin Luther King Jr.* New York: Penguin Books USA, 1993, x.

2. Young, Andrew, *An Easy Burden*. New York: HarperCollins, 1996, 233.
3. Abernathy, Ralph David, *And The Walls Came Tumbling Down*. New York: Harper and Row, 1989, 492.
4. Bennett, Lerone Jr., *What Manner of Man: A Biography of Martin Luther King Jr.*, seventh revised ed. Chicago: Johnson Publishing Co., 1989, 88.
5. Siebold, Thomas, ed., *Martin Luther King Jr. : People Who Made History*. San Diego, CA: Greenhaven Press, 2000, 142.
6. Ibid.
7. *Seattle Times*, January 16, 1994.

Nonviolence

1. Bennett, Lerone Jr., *What Manner of Man: A Biography of Martin Luther King Jr.*, seventh revised ed. Chicago: Johnson Publishing Co., 1989, 38.
2. King, Martin Luther Jr., *Stride Toward Freedom*. New York: Harper and Row, 1986, 102.
3. Washington, James M., ed., *A Testament of Hope, The Essential Writings of Martin Luther King Jr.* New York: Harper and Row, 1986, 7.
4. King, Martin Luther Jr., *Stride Toward Freedom*. New York: Harper and Row, 1986, 103.
5. King, Martin Luther Jr., *Where Do We Go From Here: Chaos Or Community?* Boston: Beacon Press, 1968, 86.
6. Phillips, Donald T., *Martin Luther King Jr. on Leadership*. New York: Warner Books, 1998, 258.
7. Washington, James M., ed., *A Testament of Hope, The Essential Writings of Martin Luther King Jr.* New York: Harper and Row, 1986, 7.
8. King, Martin Luther Jr., *Stride Toward Freedom*. New York: Harper and Row, 1986, 220.
9. Ibid., 106.
10. David, Lester, and Irene David, *Bobby Kennedy: The Making of a Folk Hero*. New York: Dodd, Mead, and Co., 1986, 305.
11. King, Martin Luther Jr., *Stride Toward Freedom*. New York: Harper and Row, 1986, 103–04.

Notes

12. King, Martin Luther Jr., *Where Do We Go From Here: Chaos Or Community?* Boston: Beacon Press, 1968, 64.

13. King, Martin Luther Jr., *Stride Toward Freedom.* New York: Harper and Row, 1986, 102.

14. Phillips, Donald T., *Martin Luther King Jr. on Leadership.* New York: Warner Books, 1998, 68.

15. King, Martin Luther Jr., *Where Do We Go From Here: Chaos Or Community?* Boston: Beacon Press, 1968, 139.

16. Phillips, Donald T., *Martin Luther King Jr. on Leadership.* New York: Warner Books, 1998, 67.

17. King, Martin Luther Jr., *The Trumpet of Conscience.* New York: Harper and Row, 1967, 70.

18. King, Martin Luther Jr., *Stride Toward Freedom.* New York: Harper and Row, 1986, 103.

19. Ibid., 188.

Inspiration

1. Carson, Clayborne, ed., *The Autobiography of Martin Luther King Jr.* New York: Warner Books, 1998, 352–353.

2. King, Martin Luther Jr., *The Trumpet of Conscience.* New York: Harper and Row, 1967, 76.

3. King, Martin Luther Jr., *The Strength to Love.* Philadelphia: Fortress Press, 1981, 93.

4. King, Martin Luther Jr., *Where Do We Go From Here: Chaos Or Community?* Boston: Beacon Press, 1968, 97.

5. Ibid., 99.

6. Ibid., 127–28.

7. King, Martin Luther Jr., *The Strength to Love.* Philadelphia: Fortress Press, 1981, 27.

8. King, Martin Luther Jr., *Where Do We Go From Here: Chaos Or Community?* New York: Harper and Row, 1967, 181.

9. Carson, Clayborne, ed., *The Autobiography of Martin Luther King Jr.* New York: Warner Books, 1998, 203.

10. Ibid.

11. Colaiaco, James A., *Martin Luther King Jr.: Apostle of Militant Nonviolence*. New York: St. Martin's Press, 1993, 74.
12. Carson, Clayborne, ed., *The Autobiography of Martin Luther King Jr.* New York: Warner Books, 1998, 342.
13. Phillips, Donald T., *Martin Luther King Jr. on Leadership*. New York: Warner Books, 1998, 330.
14. Ibid.
15. King, Martin Luther Jr., *Where Do We Go From Here: Chaos Or Community?* Boston: Beacon Press, 1968, 131.
16. Ibid., 97.
17. King, Martin Luther Jr., *The Trumpet of Conscience*. New York: Harper and Row, 1967, 55.
18. Ibid., 72.
19. King, Martin Luther Jr., *Where Do We Go From Here: Chaos Or Community?* Boston: Beacon Press, 1968, 97.
20. Ibid.
21. Phillips, Donald T., *Martin Luther King Jr. on Leadership*. New York: Warner Books, 1998, 330.

Cuisine

1. Young, Andrew, *An Easy Burden*. New York: HarperCollins, 1996, 233.
2. Abernathy, Ralph David, *And the Walls Came Tumbling Down*. New York: Harper and Row, 1989, 470.

King's Oratory

1. *Seattle Times*, January 16, 1994.
2. Ibid.
3. Ibid.
4. Bennett, Lerone Jr., *What Manner of Man: A Biography of Martin Luther King Jr.*, seventh revised ed. Chicago: Johnson Publishing Co., 1989, 27.

Love

1. Phillips, Donald T., *Martin Luther King Jr. on Leadership*. New York: Warner Books, 1998, 67.

Notes

2. Ibid., 68.
3. Ibid.
4. King, Martin Luther Jr., *The Strength to Love*. Philadelphia: Fortress Press, 1981, 50.
5. Ibid., 53.
6. Lewis, John, with Michael D'Orso, *With the Wind: A Memoir of the Movement*. New York: Simon and Schuster, 1998, 86.
7. King, Martin Luther Jr., *The Strength to Love*. Philadelphia: Fortress Press, 1981, 54.
8. Carson, Clayborne, ed., *The Autobiography of Martin Luther King Jr.* New York: Warner Books, 1998, 60.
9. Ibid.
10. Ibid., 63.
11. King, Martin Luther Jr., *Where Do We Go From Here: Chaos Or Community?* Boston: Beacon Press, 1968, 90.
12. Ibid., 37.
13. Ibid.
14. King, Martin Luther Jr., *The Strength to Love*. Philadelphia: Fortress Press, 1981, 17.
15. Ibid., 153.
16. King, Martin Luther Jr., *The Trumpet of Conscience*. New York: Harper and Row, 1967, 74.

Humor
1. King, Martin Luther Jr., *Stride Toward Freedom*. New York: Harper and Row, 1986, 129.
2. Young, Andrew, *An Easy Burden*. New York: HarperCollins, 305.
3. Siebold, Thomas, ed., *People Who Made History: Martin Luther King Jr.* San Diego, CA: Greenhaven Press, 2000, 13.
4. Abernathy, Ralph, *And the Walls Came Tumbling Down*. New York: Harper and Row, 1989, 468.
5. Young, Andrew, *An Easy Burden*. New York: HarperCollins, 332.

King's Last Day

1. Young, Andrew, *An Easy Burden*. New York: HarperCollins, 463.
2. Phillips, Donald T., *Martin Luther King Jr. on Leadership*. New York: Warner Books, 1998, 331.
3. King, Martin Luther Jr., *The Strength to Love*. Philadelphia: Fortress Press, 1981, 124.
4. Ibid., 122.
5. Ibid., 113.
6. Carson, Clayborne, ed., *The Autobiography of Martin Luther King Jr.* New York: Warner Books, 1998, 357.
7. *Seattle Times*, December 1995.
8. King, Martin Luther Jr., *The Strength to Love*. Philadelphia: Fortress Press, 1981, 96.

A Final Tribute

1. Julian Bond, "Remember the Man and Hero, Not Just Half the Dream," *Seattle Times*, April 4, 1993, posted on seattletimes.com.
2. Oates, Stephen B., *Let the Trumpet Sound: A Life of Martin Luther King Jr.* New York: HarperCollins, 1982, 497.
3. Bobby Kennedy speech delivered in Indianapolis, Indiana, on April 4, 1968, and posted on mtsu.edu.
4. CNN.com, January 18, 1998.
5. seattletimes.com.
6. *Seattle Times*, April 4, 1993, posted on seattletimes.com.
7. Young, Andrew, *An Easy Burden*. New York: HarperCollins, 469.
8. Ayres, Alex, ed., *The Wisdom of Martin Luther King Jr.* New York: Penguin Books USA, 1993, x.